Southern
Messenger
Poets

DAVE SMITH, EDITOR

the house of blue light

the house of blue light

poems

DAVID KIRBY

Louisiana State University Press   Baton Rouge
MM

Designer: Barbara Neely Bourgoyne
Typeface: Adobe Garamond
Printer and Binder: Thomson-Shore, Inc.

Library of Congress Cataloging-in-Publication Data

Kirby, David, 1944–
    The house of blue light : poems / David Kirby.
        p. cm. — (Southern messenger poets)
    ISBN 0-8071-2616-0 (cloth : alk. paper) — ISBN 0-8071-2617-9 (pbk. : alk. paper)
    I. Title. II. Series.

PS3561.I66 H68 2000
811'.54—dc21

                                                                    00-040571

The author offers grateful acknowledgment to the editors of the following journals, in which some of these poems first appeared: *Five Points:* "The Exorcist of Notre-Dame," "Meetings with Remarkable Men," "An Otherwise Mediocre Film," "Roman Polanski's Cookies"; *Gulf Coast:* "Moderation Kills (Excusez-Moi, Je Suis Sick as a Dog)"; *Kenyon Review:* "Dear Derrida"; *The Ledge:* "Catholic Teenager from Hell Goes to Italy"; *Mangrove:* "Heat Lightning"; *Northwest Review:* "A Little Cough Syrup," "Tige Watley's Whoah"; *Parnassus:* "At the Grave of Harold Goldstein"; *River Styx:* "For Men Only"; and *Southern Review:* "The House of Blue Light," "My Dead Dad," "Strip Poker," "Teacher of the Year."
    "At the Grave of Harold Goldstein" also appeared in *Best American Poetry 2000.* "My Dead Dad" also appeared in *Pushcart Prize XXV.*

for Roger Lathbury

CONTENTS

in a little silver boat

we've been waiting for you

STRIP POKER

I'm giving blood and looking at a magazine photo
of bosomy Ava Gardner next to that squirt Sinatra
     and remember saying, "Want to play strip poker?"
to my mom when I was eight because I thought it was a game,
     not a way to get naked, and was ready to put on
lots of layers that hot July evening—
     pj's, raincoat, my patrolboy's belt
with the badge I was so proud of—and figuring
     my mom would do the same with her clothes:

     the cotton dresses she taught fifth grade in
over the jeans and boots she wore for gardening
     and, on top of everything, the long coat she wore
when she went out with my dad on cool nights
     and the ratty mink stole her rich sister had given her.
My dad looked up from his newspaper, looked down again.
     My mother looked up from her book, looked down again,
looked up again, said, "No, thank you, darling,"
     which is how it was in our house:

     no yelling, no explanation, even,
just the assumption that you were a smart kid,
     you could figure things out on your own,
like "no, thanks" meant "no, but thank you anyway"
     and not "zero thanks," or that the K-9 corps
was so-called because K-9 = canine,
     i.e., wasn't just some arbitrary government code—
which is good, I guess, because if people
     aren't constantly explaining stuff to you

     when you're a kid, then you grow up mentally active,
though also doubting everything,
     even yourself, because if you're the one
who comes up with the answers,
     then what the hell good are they?

Which is the kind of thing that led
        Kafka to ask, "What have I in common
with the Jews? I have hardly anything
        in common with myself,"

        and might have led Stalin to ask,
"What have I in common with other human beings,"
        only he was too busy coming up
with rules such as this one for the Union
        of Soviet Composers:
"The main attention of the Soviet composer
        must be directed toward
the victorious progressive principles of reality, toward all
        that is heroic, bright, and beautiful."

        But what about all that is cowardly,
dull, and ugly? Tightrope-walker Karl Wallenda:
        "To be on the wire is life;
the rest is waiting." But there's much more waiting
        than wire-walking, so what are we
supposed to do when we're on the ground? Someone,
        not Henry James, I think,
but one of those Henry James kind of guys—
        cultured, reticent,

        well-off but not too—said a gentleman
was a person who never knowingly made
        anyone else uncomfortable, which is a good idea,
although one you can take too far,
        because one of those old smart Greeks, maybe Sophocles,
said it was better never to be born,
        and think how comfortable that would make everybody,
because if you weren't born, you couldn't bother anyone,
        especially yourself!

        "Are you a runner, Mr. Kirby?" asks Melba
the blood-bank nurse, who has two fingers
        on my right wrist and one eye on her watch

and the other on me, who says,
        no, he's not a runner, though he does a lot
of yard work, and why does she want to know,
        and Melba says, "Because you have a pulse of fifty,
and if you have a pulse of fifty and you're not a runner,
        often that means you're dead,"

        which, sooner or later,
I will be, will be naked again, sans pj's,
        raincoat, belt and badge, everything.
The blood leaps from a vein in my elbow,
        pools in a plastic sack, and I'm a little whiter
than I was when I read that Ava Gardner said,
        "Deep down, I'm pretty superficial"—
deep down, Ava darling, we're all pretty superficial,
        and beautiful, too, in or out of our clothes.

A LITTLE COUGH SYRUP

I tell Richard, my 403(b) guy, that I want to make a change
        in my deferred-compensation plan, and he says,
"Let me give you that 800 number so you can call the California office,"
        because, he says, if he's had a little cough syrup that day,

he could make a mistake that, thirty years from now,
        would have a client eating Alpo right out of the can,
like not even able to buy a dog dish in the big, mysterious,
        and, for that reason, scary future waiting out there somewhere

and connected to each of us by a line along which are scattered
        all the things we think we can overcome when we are as young
as I, *poseur* and shit-for-brains, was thirty years earlier
        in the chest-high gray trousers and tight purple shirt

I'd just bought at a *bodega* in Spanish Harlem, though the guy
        I look like isn't me, is, instead, a New Yorker, tough guy
full of street smarts, not a sixteen-year-old hick from Baton Rouge, LA,
        on his way back from a summer job on Cape Cod and stopping now

in the city with his friend Bertrand to make a little gas money
        for the trip home, Bertrand passing out flyers for an electronics shop
and me washing cars until I get fired for pulling off a customer's skirt
        with the vacuum cleaner and decide to spend my pay on my idea

of what a city kid wears, i.e., Shark-and-Jet attire, right down to
        the aptly named "fence-climbers" on my feet, an ensemble Nuyorican
and therefore totally outlandish on my blond and freckled body,
        but, hell, I don't want my body anymore, don't want to have anything to do

with anyone from Baton Rouge, including myself, except Bertrand,
        who apparently has a relative in every second city we pass through,
such as the man-mountain uncle in Dayton we stop in on a week later
        at seven in the morning and who speaks in a series of heh-heh chuckles

punctuated by an occasional phrase and who is just about to sit down
           to a platter of at least a dozen fried eggs and maybe twice as many
tomato slices, all of which he gives to us, saying, A-heh-heh-heh,
           dig in, boys, heh-heh-heh-heh, plenty more where that came from,

a-heh, a-heh-heh-heh, and at first I think he is laughing
           at my fab Puerto Rican vines, which he isn't, and at that moment
I want to be, not a New York street kid anymore,
           but a huge happy glutton, someone as much above it all

as the emperor Sigismund we studied in Latin II who, having made
           an error in speech and been corrected by a cardinal, replied,
Ego sum rex Romanus et super grammatica, or, I am king of Rome
           and above grammar, meaning, of course, the ablative and the pluperfect,

though what I am beginning to suspect on this long trip from the Cape
           to my mother's kitchen again is that each life has its own grammar
and that there is no point in trying to transcend yours by being
           somebody else, that if you are alive at all, you are essentially

in the same position I'd been in two days earlier in New Jersey
           at the Palisades Park I'd insisted we visit because of the song
of that name by Freddie "Boom Boom" Cannon and where I soon
           find myself spinning dizzily on the Tilt-a-Whirl and feeling

this terrible pain in the back of my head, and when I resist
           the centrifugal force long enough to lift myself and look around,
I see that everybody else has a head pad, though mine has fallen off,
           and the Tilt-a-Whirl guy is too cheap to replace it, or maybe

he'd just taken a little cough syrup that day, the result being
           that a rusty bolt is boring into my skull, and though
I manage to pull away from time to time, sooner or later
           my head snaps back and, pow, I get another grammar lesson.

        *   *   *

You don't even need to take that syrup to mess up a life, your own
                    or someone else's: the first day on the job I now have,
the sweetest little old lady is the only person on duty in
                    the personnel office, and there are two new hires there,

me and a guy with a full beard and hair out to here, and the old lady says
                    if it's okay with us, she'll tell us both about our retirement options
at the same time, and I say okay, and the crazy-haired guy just sort of bristles,
                    and the sweet old lady says, "Now, Doctuh Kirby, we have

two retah-ment plans heah at Flah-da State, and the first does blah-blah,
                    while the second does blah-blah-blah, and which one do you want?"
And I say I'll take the one she recommends, and she says,
                    "You have made a ve'y fine choice," and then she turns to Grizzly Adams

and says, "Now how 'bout you, professuh," and he says—
                    and remember, this is 1969—"I don't give a fuck, it's all a bunch
of capitalist bullshit anyway, just put me in whichever fucking one
                    you want!" and the old lady smiles the sweetest smile and says,

"Ve'y well!" and makes a mark on his form, and I imagine her going home
                    that evening and having an Old Fashioned and some crackers and rat cheese
on the patio with her husband and saying, "Henruh, I met the rudest
                    young man today," and I also imagine young Doctor Sasquatch

hobbling back into personnel when he's seventy, and the person on duty
                    says he can't explain it, but for some reason there don't seem to be
any funds deposited into that particular account, and he's mad all over again
                    but it's, like, Milk-Bone time for him.

                    *   *   *

The last night before we get back to Baton Rouge, we pull off the highway
                    somewhere near Marksville or Cottonport because Bertrand remembers
another set of relatives, his father's great-uncle and family who live
                    on the bayou in this big sprawling house, and the great-uncle is dead,

though the great-aunt is alive, as is her mother and, incredibly,
 her grandmother, who must be three thousand years old and who,
far from having undergone the traditional desiccation of old age,
 has, over the years, fattened to a bulk that, along with her refusal

to utter a word, lends a certain mystique to her in the eyes of
 two teenaged boys, Bertrand and his Nuyorican fashion-plate friend,
who are welcomed as though expected and given étouffée and jambalaya
 and cornbread and ice cream with sliced peaches and bottle after cold,

sweaty bottle of Dixie 45 and made to tell their stories and to listen to
 those of the others, most of which center around a family member
named Uncle Junior who blows stumps for a living and who was
 complaining that very day about a helper who had left a screwdriver

on an oak stump and retreated to what he thought was a safe distance,
 though when the charge went off, the helper caught the tool "right in
the brisket," according to Junior, and had to be trucked to the clinic
 at Junior's expense, "and that was a brand-new screwdriver, too."

Then off to bed, which, for me, is a cot on the screen porch,
 where I lie awake for a long time and listen to the tree frogs singing
and the nutrias splashing and the bull alligators doing that throaty roar
 they do when they're looking for wives and, once, the child's scream

a rabbit makes when an owl's got him, and then I doze a while and wake
 and sleep again and finally wake for good just as the morning light
begins to come through the cypress trees, that dull blue glow that arrives
 a half hour before the sun itself, and when I open my eyes,

the great-aunt's enormous grandmother is standing by the cot,
 still dressed the way she'd been the night before, and staring down at me,
her eyes wet and bulging in the dimness like those of some creature
 who has come up out of the swamp for God knows what evil purpose.

My own eyes snap shut again instantly, and I lie there a good forty-five minutes,
 venturing an occasional peep at this crazy old Cajun lady looming over me

like my future, huge, silent, unfathomable, and then, suddenly, gone,
       having disappeared noiselessly between peeps. "Bertrand," I say, having

found him in a sleeping bag on the kitchen floor and now vigorously
       shaking his shoulder, "we've got to get out of here," and, sure enough,
find myself that very night in my parents' house again, and as the days
       go by, moving half-aware into preparation for my senior year

and the coming break when I go away to college and all the things
       I have to think about and do and all the advice my folks are giving me
so I won't make the same mistakes they made, though why shouldn't I,
       since I love them and want to be like them and will, whether I want to

or not, fuse the grammar of their lives with my own so far, as well as
       the parts that haven't been written yet, the half-formed subjects
and predicates still roiling in the ooze of the yet-to-come, our Caliban lives
       at once unutterable and frail.

AT THE GRAVE OF HAROLD GOLDSTEIN

I'm at a graveside service for someone I didn't know,
    a Mrs. Goldiner, the mother of my friend Maxine,
who is sitting with her sisters Jill and Andrea
    and sniffling a little as the rabbi, who calls himself
"Rabbi" when he phones the house, as in
    "This is Rabbi" ("Don't you think that's primal?"
Maxine will say later. "Don't you expect someone
    with a robe and a staff in his hand?"),

is saying how the dead woman grew up in Pennsylvania
    and went to New York and worked for Saks Fifth Avenue
and met her future husband at a party, and by now
    I'm daydreaming in sepia about the Lower East Side
and anxious first-generation immigrant parents
    and yeshiva boys and pigtailed girls in gingham dresses
and storefronts and pushcarts and Model-A Fords,

when suddenly I realize that I'm standing by the grave
    of someone I did know, Harold Goldstein, who was
the dean of the library school at the university
    where I work and whom I liked a lot, a person
"of pure character," as his headstone says, and,
    continuing with the engraver's characteristic disregard
of punctuation, "lofty aims / life rich in generous
    regard for others, and devotion to publicity,"

and I think, Well, that's one thing we had
    in common, and then I look again, and of course
it says, "devotion to public duty," not publicity,
    and for a moment I blush to think not only
of my exaggerated self-love but also my eagerness
    to associate myself with someone as fine as
Harold Goldstein, who, as far as I could tell,

was pure, lofty, generous, and so on,
 whereas I, even in my late forties, am different
only in degree rather than kind from
 the self-appointed JD of *annum Domini* 1961,
tough-guy-in-his-own-mind-only
 who had but dreamed of genuine juvenile delinquency,
dreamed of being bad enough
 to be sent by his parents to all-boys Catholic High,

which was part religious school and part
 minimum-security detention center, since it contained
not only the sons of the faithful but also
 most of the fuck-ups from the public schools,
who were now concentrated under one roof
 and therefore in a position to learn additional vices
as well as pass on the ones they had already mastered

to such a one as I, who would digest far more
 of the world's nastiness were he to be yanked summarily
from the cookies-and-milk milieu of Baton Rouge High
 and set down without preamble among the brawlers,
purse snatchers, serial masturbators, and teen alcoholics
 of dear old CHS, one of whom was the inestimable
Riley Tucker of this narrator's youth, which Riley,
 having revealed his penchant for crime even earlier,

had been sentenced to terms in Catholic
 Elementary as well as Catholic Junior High
and by now was specializing in the theft,
 joyriding in, and abandonment of General Motors
vehicles—the bigger, the better, since his ordinary mode
 of transport was not only shamefully legal
but small, a Renault with the engine in the back

and a two-note town-and-country horn
 that his father had given up for the Buick
that better matched his position in life,
 whereas the Renault only mocked Riley's outlaw status;

worse, one of the conditions of his sentence
        was that he had to take his sister to
her all-girl school, St. Agnes, which she had
        to attend as a parallel to Riley's incarceration,

though eventually he persuaded his mom to alternate days
        with him so we could join the track team, our workouts
consisting less of stretching and running laps and more
        of eating Hershey bars and drinking 7-Ups and smoking
Riley's supply of shoplifted Chesterfields and Kools.
        This one day I needed a ride home,
so after school I set out with Riley in the Renault,

and when we got to St. Agnes, the girls were waiting
        out front, most of them having undone the top buttons
of their blouses and pulled their plaid skirts up
        and lain out on the lawn to enjoy the last of the sun
while they waited for their rides and listened to
        the ineffectual cluckings of the elderly nun
whose job it was to see them off the premises,
        and what happened next was that Riley

decided to "cut some maneuvers" in the Renault
        so the girls could see how fabulous we were,
only in the course of the zigs and the zags
        and the zips, Riley spun the wheel so hard
that we found ourselves on the wrong side
        of the little French car's notoriously high center
of gravity, and we ended upside-down in the parking lot,

the Renault teetering nicely on its roof as Riley
        and I huddled on our heads and shoulders and watched
Riley's sister get in their mother's car—where did *she* come from?—
        and vanish. Standing at the grave of Harold Goldstein,
I can still see Riley's upside-down mother
        giving us a single disgusted glance and then
driving away slowly, her car gliding as though fixed
        to some futuristic monorail.

Suddenly there is a commotion: Rabbi has alluded to the fact
        that Maxine's sister Andrea is pregnant
by her husband Charles, only Andrea too has been daydreaming
        and thinks Rabbi has said "her husband Al,"
who is actually Maxine and Jill and Andrea's late father,
        so Andrea says, "Charles! Charles!" and the others say,
"Rabbi said 'Charles,' Andrea," and Andrea calms down.

What was Riley's mother doing at St. Agnes anyway?
        Obviously either she or he had got the day wrong,
but I'll never know, because the totaled Renault
        was towed and forgotten, and I,
guilty by association, walked everywhere for a year,
        though usually only down to the corner,
where I waited for Riley to come by in his latest acquisition,
        the theft of which I was also an accessory to,

I suppose, even if we were never caught. My crimes are
        little ones these days, but I guess we should all
do the best we can, so it's probably good to have
        this kind of accident, by which I mean the unplanned
rediscovery of a person like Harold Goldstein,
        of which the world needs more, not less,
and whose example I have resolved to emulate

as much as my below-average character and mediocre aims
        permit, even though his way, the right-side-up way,
is not especially aesthetic, but why even think about
        aesthetics when things are falling apart all around you
and death and misunderstanding are on every side?
        Then again, in *Stardust Memories*, when Woody Allen
asks these wise space aliens who visit Earth
        if he shouldn't be performing more good deeds,

they tell him that if he really wants to serve humanity,
        he should tell funnier jokes—wait, that's *my* duty,
I think, that's my public duty! Because sooner or later,

we all turn upside down: you're zipping along nicely,
a hotshot, and everybody's checking you out, when boom,
over you go. And look! There goes your mother!
She's driving away slowly across the ceiling of the world.

DEAR DERRIDA

My new grad-school roommates and I are attending
       our first real lecture, which has gone okay,
we guess, since none of us understands it,
            when one of our professors rises,
a somewhat prissy fellow
       with a mild speech impediment,
and says he takes issue with the speaker's tone,
            which he characterizes as one of "sar, sar,"
and here he raises his voice a little,
       "sar, sar, sar," and wipes his mouth

with a handkerchief, "sar," and turns red
            and screams, "sar, sar, sar—DAMN EET!—sarcasm!"
The four of us look at each other
       as if to say, Hmmmm, nothing like this
at the cow colleges we went to!
            After that, whenever we'd spill our coffee
or get a sock stuck in the vacuum cleaner,
       we'd look at the mess ruefully
       and say, "Da, da, da—SARCASM!—damn eet!"

Our lives were pretty tightly sealed,
       and if we weren't in class or the library,
either we spent our time in wordplay
            or cooking: what with girlfriends
and passersby, we always had a pot
       of water boiling on the back of the stove
(It's like you're ready to deliver babies,
            somebody said once), either for spaghetti
or sausages, though one evening Chris,
       the English student from England, came by

for a sausage supper, and after he left,
            we ran up on the roof to pelt him
with water balloons, though when we did,

he fell down as though he'd been shot,
and one of us said, Jeez, what's wrong
                with Chris, and somebody else said,
You know, Chris eats nothing but sausage,
                and a third party said, Hmm,
        maybe we ought to vary our diet a little.

        And that was our life: school, the boiled messes
        we made on that stove, and hanging around
that crummy apartment talking about,
                I don't know, Dr. Mueller's arm,
I guess, which hung uselessly
        by his side for reasons no one
fathomed—polio, maybe, or some
                other childhood disease—though Paul
said he thought it was made of wood.
        Can't be made of wood, said Michael,

you can see his hand at the end
                of it, to which Paul replied,
Yeah, but you can have a wooden arm
        and a real hand, can't you?
And that was what our life was like,
                because mainly we just sat around
and speculated like crazy while
                the snow piled up outside,
        so much so that by the time spring came,

        I'd had it, so I moved out of there and in with Grant
        and Brian and Poor Tom, who were philosophy
students but also genuine bad asses,
        believe it or not, because at that time
you more or less had to be an existentialist,
        i.e., tough, and not a deconstructionist,
which was a few years down the road yet
                and which would have left everyone
paralyzed, since all texts
        eventually cancel themselves out.

Of the new roomies, I hit it off best
                with Grant, who became one of the big-brother
types I seemed to be looking for at that period in my life,
                and in fact he rescued me
on more than one occasion, such as the time I was talking
                to a local girl outside a bar
called Jazz City and her three brothers
                decided to "teach me a lesson" and would have
                if Grant hadn't punched one of them

                across the hood of a parked car, or the night
                he and I were in this other place where
a biker gang called Quantrill's Raiders
                hung out and into which wandered
a well-dressed couple so unaware
                of their surroundings that they asked the bartender
to please make them some hot toddies,
                which set everybody to laughing,
only the Quantrills decided we were laughing at them
                and jumped up to "teach us a lesson"

and would have, too, if Grant had not thrown
                a table at them and dragged me
out of there to dive behind some garbage cans
                and choke on our own laughter
while the drunk, fucked-up bikers howled
                and swore and punched each other since they
couldn't punch us. All this was therapy,
                I figured, since grad school was stressful enough
                to send three people I knew to the clinic

                with barbiturate overdoses (two made it,
                one didn't), and I'm not even listing here
all the divorces I know of that were directly
                attributable to that constant pressure
to be the best, be publishable, hireable,
                lovable, that came from professors and sweethearts
and parents but mainly from ourselves,

as though each of us were two people,
a good and capable slave, on the one hand,
        and, on the other, a psychotic master

who either locked us up with our pots
            of boiling water or sent us out to dance
with the devil in the streets of Baltimore.
        That year magi appeared from the east:
Jacques Lacan, Tzvetan Todorov,
            Roland Barthes, and Jacques Derrida
brought their Saussurean strategies
            to the Hopkins conference on "The Language
of Criticism and the Sciences of Man,"

            where they told us that all language
        is code and thus separate from reality,
and therefore everything
            is a text as long as there is nothing
more than this half-conscious
        linguistic interplay between perceiver
and perceived, which is another way
            of saying that language is the only reality
or at least the only one that counts.
        As different as these thinkers are,

each was telling us that there is no us:
            that cultural structures
or the media or Western thought
        or the unconscious mind
or economic systems make us
            what we are or what we seem to be, since,
in fact, we are not, which isn't such bad news,
            if you think about it, because it means
        we don't have to take ourselves so seriously.

            Derrida and company make it impossible
        for anyone today to read a book
as he had before, but we didn't know that then.

Grant didn't, that's for sure;
four years later, he put a gun in his mouth
        and blew the back of his skull off,
and sometimes it makes me sad
                when I think of how long it takes
for new ideas to catch on, because,
        yeah, deconstruction might have saved us.

CATHOLIC TEENAGER FROM HELL GOES TO ITALY

Jock DuBois found out in our senior year
        that one out of every seven Americans was Catholic,
so he figured if each of us would rise up
        on a secret signal and kill seven non-Catholics,
we could take over the whole country in,
        like, three or four minutes, a hypothesis
that cost us several jobs,
        since Jock couldn't stop talking about his plan,
and even devoutly Catholic bosses
        had no desire to see their employees
doff their brightly-colored paper caps
        or throw down their mops and brooms
and start killing customers who had come in
        for a burger, shake, and biggie fry,
not to have their throats cut by pimply fanatics.

That didn't stop Jock from talking,
        even though I said the plan might work in America,
but what about the rest of the world,
        including our immediate neighbors?
It just didn't seem like something
        the Canadians would take lying down.
I wasn't sure I wanted Catholics
        to run the world anyway, even though
JFK had just been elected president,
        and some people were saying he was already
getting secret orders from the Vatican,
        and others were passing out what they called
"Kennedy quarters," the ones
        where Washington is wearing a papal skullcap
they'd painted on with red nail polish.

A year later, none of it mattered.
        Oswald slew Kennedy in Dallas,
and my faith died, too, shot in the head

by college, by pretty girls and cheap beer
and philosophy professors I loved more
        than my own parents, who wept when I told them
I wasn't going to mass at St. Aloysius anymore,
        that the church had no connection with my life,
was another planet, really,
        even though it was just a mile from our house,
a miserable cavern I languished in
        every Sunday morning as I checked the exits
and listened to the shotguns racheting in my mind
        and wondered, How many guys
would I need to take over this place,

a thought I hardly have in mind this summer
        when Barbara and I stop at the church
of La Madonna delle Lacrime on a hill near Trevi
        to see Perugino's *Adoration of the Magi,*
and at the time we are the only people there
        besides this other guy and his wife,
and Barbara has taken a sketching class
        this summer and is just irritating
the living crap out of me by drawing
        virtually everything she sees—
like, we'll be having breakfast in some piazza
        and she'll use a packet of sugar
and then take a napkin and start drawing
        the empty sugar packet on it—
so, as usual, she wants to sketch the Perugino,

and I'm standing around checking out
        the other paintings, which are pretty much nothing,
and the guy comes up to me and says,
        Do you speak Italian, and I say, A little,
and he hands me a key and says,
        When you're through here, lock up
from the outside and take the key over
        to the convent next door and give it
to the blind nun who answers the bell,

and I say, So I lock the door and take the key
over to the convent and give it to
        a blind nun? and he says, Exactly,
and gets in a yellow Opel Corsa with his wife
        and drives away, so I walk back to look
at the Perugino for a while

and to look over Barbara's shoulder
        at her drawing, and she's done, like,
one of the legs of one of the Magi,
        and she says, Quit looking at me,
so I walk outside and toss the key up and catch it
        for a while and then start playing
a little game I made up in the States,
        which is to toss your keys behind your back
and over your opposite shoulder
        and catch them in front with the same hand
you used for the tossing,
        and people always like to see you do that,
because if you catch the keys, they're happy,
        and if you miss the keys, they're even happier,
only there's no one out here on this hill,

so I start thinking about the Perugino again,
        and thinking, Here I am, in charge of the future
of Italian art, or at least one considerable piece
        of it, and while I wasn't going to steal it,
I could have drawn the biggest, fattest dick
        known to mankind on one of the shepherds
or given everybody sideburns and mustaches,
        only I'm not angry at the Church
any more than I was ready to kill for it
        the way Jock DuBois had been, so that when
Barbara finally comes out and says, Let's go,
        I just lock up and go to the convent door
and ring the bell and hear the blind nun
        shout, *Eccomi!* (Here I am!)
as she bats her way down the hall

and finds the door and yanks it open
        and grabs for the key, which she misses,
because I have already moved my hand
        to where hers had been, and we do that
several times until she finally takes
        a lucky swing and grabs the key and gives me
a hearty though, now that I think about it,
        almost certainly ironic *Arrivederci!*
and we set off to Urbino,
        and that night I'm reading the paper
at a table in the Piazza Centrale
        while Barbara sketches the table next to ours,
and I see where Giulio Andreotti,
        the former prime minister now on trial
for corruption, told a journalist

that his solace came from "the old Catholic wisdom
        of the Roman people" that an aunt had taught him,
namely, (1) never overdramatize things;
        (2) everything, over time, can be fixed;
(3) keep a certain detachment from everything;
        and (4) the important things in life are very few,
and I think, well, that makes more sense
        than anything I ever heard as a boy
back at St. Aloysius, even though these truths
        didn't keep Andreotti from becoming a rascal,
but then that's the nature of wisdom,
        Catholic or otherwise. I love the Church today
for preserving all those fabulous art works,
        and even though I hope I don't have
a deathbed conversion, if I do,

and there is a heaven, I wouldn't expect to get in,
        since I serve poetry now and not God,
but maybe I could be, I don't know, *transferred*
        to Perugino's fresco, sort of slowly starting
to appear in outline and then more and more,
        and not as one of the Wise Men, of course,

or even a shepherd, but just, you know,
    a lout, neighborhood guy who hears a commotion
and goes over to see what's going on,
    and there is this mother and father,
and there's an ass and a cow and a dog,
    and in the middle of it all,
there's this baby, and the mother is thinking,
    Maybe he'll grow up to be somebody,
a rabbi or a healer or just a person everyone loves,

but then what if people don't understand him
    and try to hurt him or even kill him,
and she'd look around, and her eyes
    would meet mine, and I wouldn't say anything,
but I'd give her a look that would say,
    I can't help you, lady, I couldn't get anybody
to be my friend in high school
    except Jock DuBois, who wanted
to kill the non-Catholics,
    and she'd be thinking, We're all non-Catholics here,
and the father would be thinking,
    We'll head toward Jerusalem,
there's work there, things will be better,
    and the baby would be thinking,
This is going to be one long day.

THE HOUSE OF BLUE LIGHT

Little Richard comes on the TV at Gold's Gym
          and the first thing that happens is, I burst into tears,
and the second thing is, I think to myself,
                    I can't sing this music, but if I could,
I wouldn't accept a smidgen of public acclaim,

not one iota; rather, I'd be like
          19th-century French historian Fustel de Coulanges
entering a lecture hall to the applause of students
                    and saying, "Do not applaud. It is not I who speak,
but history which speaks through me,"

and as I distract myself from my sorrow with this thought,
          pert *Today* show host Katie Couric
tries to cut Little Richard off,
                    tries to get the camera on herself so she can go on
with the program, so she waves the crew back

and walks toward them to fill the lens and get away
          from Little Richard's hullabaloo, which is king-sized:
he's saying, "Turn me up! Turn me up!"
                    and then, "All the beautiful women say, 'Woo woo!'"
and the women do say "Woo woo!" and they are beautiful,

that crone there, this four-hundred-pounder,
          and then he says, "All the ol' ugly men say, 'Unnh!'"
and the men do say "Unnh!" and they are ugly,
                    they're beasts, the stock brokers in their power ties,
even the slim, almost girlish delivery boys

are fat and hairy and proud to be that way,
          proud to be selfish and to take big craps,
and I'm crying and not sure whether I'm one
                    of the beautiful ones or the ugly,
and when I tell Barbara about this later,

she says, "It's an emotional time for you,
        what with Ian going away to college,"
and I see what she means,
            because at least part of my Gold's Gym sorrow
is due to the fact that tomorrow I'll say good-bye

to this boy I've had a steak-and-egg breakfast with
        practically every Saturday morning of his life,
and now he's going away, which he should,
            though why Little Richard would trigger my tears,
I have no idea, except, come to think of it,

for the strong, indeed necessary, tie between
        pop music and sentiment, as evidenced by the last time
I boohooed like a li'l weiner while listening to pop songs,
            which was after Roy Orbison had died
and, as part of a tribute show, the DJ had played,

not only Roy Orbison singing "Danny Boy,"
        an Irish father's farewell to his only son
when he goes off to fight in the foreign wars,
            but also the seldom-heard reply, which is the song
Danny Boy sings at his father's graveside when he comes back

and finds that, irony of ironies,
        while he has survived sabre blow and cannon fire,
Old Age, the surest of Death's warriors,
            has crept up on his dad and cut him down
as lethally as any of the English King's artillerymen,

and now I see Ian in his farmboy's worsteds,
        leaning on his musket and salting the stones
of my grave with his bitter tears. . . .
            My son, me, Little Richard, Roy Orbison:
it's a mishmash, for sure—

certainly it's a step into the House of Blue Light,
        the place where Miss Molly rocks

and that is not a house of prostitution,
              which would involve a light
of a different color altogether, but a fun house,

a good-time house, yet a house where
              the unexpected occurs, sort of like that place
Muhammad Ali called "the near room,"
              whose door would open in the middle of a round,
and part of Ali would be whaling the tar

out of an opponent and part would be looking
              into that room, where he'd see orange alligators
playing saxophones and dancing snakes
              with green hats on their heads,
and he'd want to go in there, want to party

with these bebop reptiles and groove-ball amphibians,
              when suddenly whup whup whup whup! his opponent
would remind him what he was there for,
              and Ali would have to whupwhupwhupwhupwhupwhup!
and take care of business real fast

and shower and have a news conference
              and then go home and wonder what he saw
in that room there with all that crazy stuff in it,
              including some things he's seen before
and some he's never seen and some he hopes to see again

and some he can't bear to think about
              even though he's home now, got his feet up
on the Danish Modern coffee table and a nice cold glass
              of fruit juice in his hand.
He's been *some*where, that's for sure!

He's been on an "expedition,"
              a word I recently heard pronounced
as "eks-pay-DEE-shone" by an Italian biologist

who was telling me about his latest trip to Antarctica
and who is probably the last person to have said

this word to my face since my brother Albert
   forty-five years ago when I was seven and he ten
and we used to play this game called African Ranger
     in the woods that surrounded our parents' house,
the one we had to sell when my parents got too old

to keep it up, the two sons talking on the porch
   as the mother sweeps and tidies and the father,
who has not cried at anything since the death
     of his own parents decades earlier, sobs in the study
as he says good-bye to his books, and it is late afternoon

in the early days of winter, and there is no part of the world
   gloomier than the bayou country at that time of the year,
and Albert says to me, "Want to play African Ranger?"
     and it takes me a minute to remember the game,
which consisted of starting out on an "expedition"

but soon turned into two shirtless boys shooting blunt arrows
   into each other's hides, and I say, "Nope,"
and he says, "Me, either," and the last piece of light
     falls out of the sky, and it's dark out there,
the woods are black; you could walk into them, if you wanted,

and a little path would take you farther and farther
   from your old life, and soon you'd see this cottage,
and there'd be music coming out of it, and you'd look in,
     and Little Richard would be there and Ali
and Roy Orbison and yourself when you were a child

but also a teenager and a young man, too,
   and everybody'd be talking and laughing,
and somebody would look up and see you as you are now,
     and they'd all wave and say,
Hey there, we've been waiting for you, come on in.

she too dreams of her lover

AN OTHERWISE MEDIOCRE FILM

At the Odéon metro stop today there is a poster
        for a movie called *Pédale Douce,* which looks like
one of those silly French sex farces in which
        a gay character has to pretend to be straight
in order to fool a boss or rich relative

and ends up being so straight that he offends
        this important person with his machismo
and so has to go the other way again,
        though of course this time he also goes too far
and so creates a whole series of new messes,

and on the poster someone has written *"un film stupide*
        fait par des stupides pour vous faire plus stupide
que vous y êtes maintenant,"
        or "a stupid film made by stupid people
to make you more stupid than you are now,"

and I think, Boy, I sure have seen
        a bunch of those in my time, because
sooner or later I think I pretty much see them all,
        catching the good ones with La Barbara
at the Miracle on Sunday afternoons

and the rest on video or cable,
        though one of my favorite movie habits is to work
until about four and then, instead of taking a nap,
        catch a matinee, usually of something not quite
good enough to warrant rapt attention anyway,

because I love to doze off
        and wake up to people pounding the crap
out of each other in some saloon
        or leaping onto a plane in flight
so they can neutralize the terrorists

and land safely, though both pilot
        and copilot are dead and the only one
who can fly is a seven-year-old
            who's just started taking lessons
so he can break the youngest-pilot record,

and even these movies often have a scene
        or an exchange between two characters
or a word said a certain way
            or maybe just a facial expression
that you'll not only remember for years

but use in a way that changes your life
        for the better, even though
it's "an otherwise mediocre film,"
            which is a phrase that occurs in
André Bazin's *Qu'est-ce Que Le Cinéma?*

or *What Is the Cinema?* in English,
        though I prefer the French version,
because after you see a real baffler
            and the house lights have come up
and you have no idea what you've just seen,

if you say, What is the cinema? to your friend,
        he'll wonder what the hell you're talking about,
whereas if you say, *Qu'est-ce que le cinéma?*
            he'll laugh and say, Beats me, and the two of you
can have a drink and try to figure it out.

Bazin's example of "an otherwise mediocre film"
        is *Where No Vultures Fly,* a movie about a young couple
in Africa whose child goes into the bush
            and finds a lion cub and carries it home,
stalked by the lioness, which scene

is shot in montage—lioness/child,
        lioness/child—until they arrive back at camp,

where the horrified parents see the angry lioness
                    about to spring upon the oblivious cubnapper,
only this part is shown in the same full shot!

Trickery is abandoned as we watch the father
          order his son to stand still, put the cub down,
and start forward again, slowly! Whereupon
                    the lioness retrieves the cub and moves off
into the bush as the audience lets out

a collective sigh of relief and settles back
          to watch the rest of the movie,
which apparently is fairly awful.
                    And while I like the movies as a whole
and am happiest when I forget who I am,

sometimes I wonder if we don't get
          the best use of them when we're watching
an otherwise mediocre film and see something
                    in it we want to lift out the way a man
with a little silver knife might prise an oyster

from its shell and let it slide down his throat
          and think, Ah, heaven, just before he tosses
the shell on the pile before him and wipes
                    his hands on his pants and sniffs his fingers
with a look of both gratification and disgust,

and this reminds me of that beautiful
          little fishing village where Marlon Brando
and his gang hole up in *One-Eyed Jacks*
                    after Karl Malden has horsewhipped Brando
and broken his gun hand with a rifle butt,

and it's the prettiest place in the world,
          a perfect spot to rest and get healthy again
and plan your next robbery and your revenge, too,

only gang member Ben Johnson can't stand it,
can't stand the sun and the waves

and the fresh, wholesome diet,
      so he keeps referring
to the beautiful little village
          as "this puke hole" and "this manure pile,"
and that's what I do sometimes

when things are going so well
      that, instead of angering the gods
by saying, Oh, boy, this is wonderful,
          or God, I love our life together,
I'll hook my thumbs in my belt

and pretend to scuff my boots
      and say, I reckon I've had it up to here
with this manure pile,
          or If I ever see this puke hole again
I reckon it'll be too soon for me,

and usually La Barbara just gives me a peck
      on the cheek and says, See you later, Ben,
though sometimes she'll get in the mood
          and say, Just get the hell off my deck,
you tub of guts, or maybe You know,

you're lookin' to get your back busted, sonny,
      and I'm the gal who takes care of them kind
of things around here, which, *mutatis mutandis,*
          is what Slim Pickens says to Marlon Brando
much earlier in the same movie.

Here's Stanley Cavell, in *Must We Mean What We Say?:*
      "If a person were shown a film of an ordinary whole day
in his life, he would go mad." True,
          because an ordinary whole day on film would appear
as a single dull continuum, whereas when we are living

said o.w.d., it is more often than not as much fun,
         if not more, than a barrel of monkeys, the monkeys
being the little pieces of what we are doing
                  at the time but also what we remember from books
we've read and smart parties we've attended

and conversations we've had
         with our parents and teachers and other sages,
including total strangers,
                  along with a great deal of sheer crap,
including the little gems

from the otherwise mediocre films
         we've seen, shiny mosaic tiles
that say nothing on their own
                  yet make part of a picture
that, you think, might make sense

once you actually finish it
         but at least is a lot of fun to work on
while you're doing it. Another critic,
         Carol Clover, wrote a wonderful essay
in which she says—and this is great, I really love this—

"the processes by which a certain image
         (but not another) filmed in a certain way
(but not another) causes one person's (but not another's)
                  pulse to race finally remains a mystery—
not only to critics and theorists but even,

to judge from interviews and the trial-and-error
         (and baldly imitative) quality of the films themselves,
to the people who make the product,"
                  or, in other words, that movie people
make movies the way the rest of us make our lives,

putting all these little pieces together
         sort of briskly and without a great deal

of forethought, thinking from time to time
           that there should be or at least could be
some coherence to the whole thing,

though that doesn't really matter
           as long as you've had a good day,
one that you started with
           a cup of strong coffee and then wrote something,
not *War and Peace,* exactly,

but a good paragraph or sentence, even,
           and after that taught a class
in which the students were lively and chatty
           and laughed at your jokes,
and after that you had a good lunch with your friends,

followed by a short nap and then some yard work, say,
           or a walk in the neighborhood,
and then the rewriting of that thing
           or that part of a thing you wrote earlier,
then reading, then dinner and a half bottle

of a decent red with the one you love, then a film,
           even a mediocre one—not that you'd know,
since you'll probably sleep through at least
           some of it, considering the kind of day you've had,
with the excellent parts but the stupid ones as well,

for surely either you will be stupid or others
           will be stupid for you, and here I think of a friend
who was playing a prostitute in a movie, and she asked
           the director, Are you going to give me a costume?
and he said, No, just wear your regular clothes.

The image of a drunken Melville beating and pushing his
wife Elizabeth down a flight of stairs has imprinted itself
on my mind's eye and caused me to hate him for abusing
her. Whether it happened or not, I know it is possible.
—Nancy Fredricks, *Melville's Art of Democracy*

My own heroes are not Andrew Jackson or John Bunyan
        or Cervantes but people I already know,
like Officer John Moore, the little skinny yellow-eyed guy
        who used to be what was called a "prize fighter"
(if you asked him, he'd think about it a little bit and then say
        his biggest match was for $10,000 in 1947 against
Wild Bill Kelly) and who now writes parking tickets
        for the football players who leave their Broncos
in the handicapped spaces outside the Williams Building
        every day so they don't have to walk far
to the desks where they'll drowse
        through my Contemporary Poetry class,

and believe me, these behemoths are not too particular
        about what they say to Officer John when they catch him
in the fulfillment of his duties, but since,
        chin in hand, I've been watching him from my window
for years as he writes those tickets, he must be
        good at it, i.e., must be pleasing to his master,
the chief, so one day I say to him, "Officer John,
        what's your secret," and he says, "Never stop writing,"
and I say, "Hmmm?" and he says, "Never stop writing!"
        and, in fact, he is writing a ticket
even as he is saying this to me, thereby providing
        a practical demonstration of his adage.

So was Melville a wife-beater? I hope not,
        because I love him, too, or at least I love the Melville
who ended Chapter 26 of *Moby-Dick* with this prayer:

"If, then, to meanest mariners, and renegades
and castaways, I shall hereafter ascribe
        high qualities . . . then against all
mortal critics bear me out in it, thou just Spirit
        of Equality, which hast spread one royal mantle
of humanity over all my kind! . . . Thou who,
        in all Thy mighty, earthly marchings, ever cullest
Thy selectest champions from the kingly commons;
        bear me out in it, O God!"—also a nice thought,

better than "Never stop writing!" probably,
        because a writer can certainly keep writing
the same junk over and over again,
        and here I think of another guy I like to think of,
and another boxer, too, as it turns out,
        a fellow I used to see sometimes in Baton Rouge,
a Golden Gloves champ and one even smaller
        than Officer John, like in the 105-pound-and-under
class, and he used to sit at the bar in the Pastime
        after workouts and nurse a beer, and he looked just awful,
as though he were crying, his hair a mess
        and his face red from his sparring partner's gloves,

and he'd sit there and drink that beer, and sometimes
        these bullies would pick on him, call him a faggot
and push him and push him, and then sometimes actually
        physically *push* him, whereupon this little unassuming
red-faced mosquito of a human being would step down
        carefully from that stool, and his arms would become
a blur in front of the bully's face and midsection,
        and you'd hear this faint sound, kind of like
a sewing machine in the next room, and after
        thirty seconds or so of this, the bully would
go over backwards and hit the floor of the Pastime
        and lie there like a pizza somebody had dropped,

and while I'm not in favor of beating
        the other fellow about the mandibles

as a solution to every problem, still,
        I like to think of that little mighty atom of a guy,
that pocket Hercules, and his gift to us all
        of that one element so largely absent
from our quotidian existence, i.e., surprise,
        and now I'm remembering the time I got the jolt
of my life and almost my death when I was seventeen
        and jogging at the track at LSU where my high-school team
worked out, the spotty teens mixing freely
        with the burlier college athletes,

and suddenly I hear myself go PHHRRGGMUH!
        as my hips shoot forward and my head snaps back
toward my heels: I have just been tackled by
        1958 Heisman Trophy–winning fullback Billy Cannon,
a star sprinter in the off-season and one now
        pointing at a javelin quivering in the earth
not ten feet away, the arc of which spear
        having been transected by the body
of your correspondent only seconds earlier,
        prompting the moralizing gladiator
to observe, "That ought to be a learner!"
        and it was, too, as in, Heads up, Dave!

Which just goes to show you that the author
        of *Moby-Dick* is right, there's plenty to learn
from the cops and boxers and fullbacks of this world.
        Poor Mrs. Melville! It can't have been easy
to be married to a solitary hemorrhoidal genius.
        I don't know if Officer John or the little boxer
or Billy Cannon ever married at all,
        but if they did, I hope they were heroes
to their wives as they are to me,
        though I doubt it, since for most of us
a hero has to be somebody familiar but not too.
        Herman, Herman, please be sweet to your Elizabeth.

JAMES DICKEY'S DREAM

The usual little cloud of asterisks and pound signs
        and exclamation marks is buzzing and fizzing over my head
    as I try to figure out how to start my writing day,
and just then the phone rings, and it's Michael Skube,
        the book editor of the *Atlanta Journal-Constitution,*
    and he wants me to write an "appreciation"
of the life and work of the late James Dickey,
        and I say, "I didn't know Dickey was dead,"

and Michael says, "He isn't" (and, in fact, won't be
        for another three years), "it's just that
    we like to have these things on file so that,
when the inevitable occurs, we're ready,"
        although, and my slow start this morning notwithstanding,
    I have a lot on my beer coaster at this time
in my life, so I hem and haw a bit, and Michael says,
        "That's okay, I've got another poet I can use,"

only this other poet turns out to be somebody
        who got drunk at my house a couple of years before
    and made fun of my CD collection, as though I not only
chose the title of Sinatra's *Songs for Swinging Lovers*
        but also somehow fancied myself a swingin' (i.e., not)
    hepcat when I am actually no cooler or un- than anyone else,
so I say, "Wait a minute, Michael, maybe I'm not as busy
        as I think," and so I get started on my day after all,

except that two or three hours into it,
        I'm calling Michael back and saying I'm not only
    tangling up my tenses by pretending a living man is dead
but also giving myself a major case of the creeps
        since I know Dickey is probably looking out a window
    in Columbia, SC, and thinking happily about some poem
he'd written or some deer he'd shot, and here I am writing
        phrases like "Dickey's greatest achievement was,"

so we talk a bit, and I fuss some more, and finally
   Michael tries to lighten the mood by saying, "Listen,
usually we pay on publication, but this time I'll pay
on receipt so you won't be sitting there hoping
   Dickey dies and then feeling as though you killed him
when he does," so I go back to work and finish the piece
and let it sit for a day or two and "give it a haircut" and file it
   and get paid and then forget about it for three years,

until last week, that is, when I read that Dickey
   has died and say to Barbara, "I killed James Dickey,"
and she says, "Actually, you gave him a little more life,"
and I think, hmmm, that's why we marry these smart women,
   and I go back and read what I'd written earlier,
and it's not too bad, but only because it uses
all these great self-descriptions of Dickey's,
   like the one from the 1990 interview where he says

he had an "assumed personality" like Hemingway's,
   a "big, strong, hard drinking, hard fighting" persona
that hides the "timid, cowardly" Dickey, the aesthete
who felt at home with authors like Oscar Wilde
   and Henry James, but then I think, nah, not Henry,
because I'd just read that, late in life,
James agreed to visit three Cambridge University men,
   even though he had never met any of them,

and that afterwards the novelist wrote a glowing
   thank-you note, even though he'd cut short his stay
because one of his hosts kept supplying missing words
whenever James paused to fumble for one, as he was wont to do,
   so that instead of reproving his new friend or bearing
the intrusion in silence, James preserved everyone's pleasure
by leaving earlier than planned, and I asked myself,
   Would Dickey have done this? and the answer is,

   No, he sure-God would have punched somebody right square
in the face instead! Amiability, power,

self-effacement: that's morality in James's world,
               whereas in Dickey's it's combat and archery and holding
               your liquor and taking a punch—handling yourself
       like a man, in other words, even if you've been raped
up the ass by a bunch of perverted incestuous hillbillies,
               which standard is rather far removed from the one

       represented by, say, a character like Adam Verver
               in *The Golden Bowl,* a good man whose selfless love
       of others, combined with economic power,
material conservatism, and exquisite taste, is not only
               the touchstone for Jamesian behavior but also the ideal
       out of which perhaps all books, all art, should flow,
though to say that makes me think of the remark
               Jane Smiley made about how much better it would be

       if American literature had sprung from *Uncle Tom's Cabin*
               instead of *The Adventures of Huckleberry Finn*
       and Roy Blount, Jr.'s reply that that's like saying
it would be better for people to come from heaven
               than from sex. To put it another way, there are
       no Henry James or Harriet Beecher Stowe impersonators,
though there are plenty of impersonators of Mark Twain
               and even James Dickey, including me, who saw him

       almost not give a reading here in Tallahassee in 1972,
               when he came out on stage wobbly-drunk,
       read two poems, thanked everybody for being so nice,
and got halfway to the wing before somebody barked,
               "Get back out here and read!" which he did magnificently
       and with great sound effects: wolf cries,
the sound of one hunter calling to another in a dark wood,
               the sssssssssk! of an arrow finding its target.

       He went on for a good forty minutes, seemingly as sober
               as the rest of us, and when the applause died down,
       said, "Thuh maan of words . . . has no words!"
which is pretty bombastic, but then that's James Dickey.

I was hoping for an invitation to the reception,
        but I was only a new assistant professor
and not fit company for the deans and vice-presidents
        who bore Mr. Dickey away to the country club,

        where, I heard later, he sat drinking all evening
        and grabbing at every skirt that went past,
        which is typical of the stories you hear about him
that are often pretty horrendous, even though
        they got a little less so as the years went by
        and then no worse than what you'd hear about other people
and then milder still and then downright tame
        as he began his long decline and started living more

        in the world of thought than the one of tangible reality,
        as, for instance, when he had the dream he told a friend
        about just before he died, in which he was playing
high-school football again and scored three touchdowns
        and ended up with the prettiest girl in the school
        and said to her, "This is the most beautiful day
of my life; too bad it's only a dream,"
        and she said, "Yes, but in the dream it's real."

        Henry James said of immortality that if you want it,
        then that's as good as believing in it,
        because while it's terrible knowing you're going to die,
maybe it's wonderful, too, as you say good-bye
        to the hard days, the ones that leave you so tired
        you can't even remember your name, and you go into
the dream instead, and you're a hero there,
        and everybody loves you again, and in the dream it's real.

TIGE WATLEY'S WHOAH

I'm laughing while I'm waiting in line at the FSU Credit Union
      because the woman ahead of me is talking
in this thick southern accent that reminds me of a woman
      my parents knew whose name was S-u-g,
pronounced "Shoog" and short for "Sugar," though my father
      didn't like her, so he called her "Sugh,"
rhyming with "ugh," and her husband's name (or the name
      he used) was Tige,

for Tiger, so they were Tige and "Shoog" Watley, unless
      you were talking to my father,
in which case they were Tige and "Sugh" Watley—anyway,
      at some point Tige, who was a dentist,
started drilling his receptionist in addition to the
      various molars, bicuspids, and canines
of the gentry of South Baton Rouge, and ever after
      Sug referred to the receptionist

as "Tige Watley's whoah," and even though I was only eleven,
      I used to bartend
my parents' parties in those days, and Sug would come up
      to me and say,
"This a nice pahty—is Tige Watley's whoah heah?" and I'd say,
      "Nope, not even Tige Watley!"
Because he was too embarrassed to attend, which was too bad,
      those were great parties,

Robert Penn Warren and Cleanth Brooks
      and Katherine Anne Porter
would be there, but then they could afford to be,
      because they'd behaved themselves
or at least they didn't have someone as angry as
      Sug Watley dogging them.
When asked to name the greatest French poet, André Gide said,
      "Victor Hugo, hélas!"

If Sug Watley were French, and someone said, Who's the biggest
    whore in Baton Rouge . . .
no, wait, they wouldn't say that, they'd say, Who's the most
    desirable woman in Baton Rouge,
she'd say, "Tige Watley's whoah—hélas!" And while I'm having
    a good chuckle
as I remember all this, suddenly—holy shit!—
    my blood runs cold

as I see this harridan I know teetering on high heels
    as she flies full tilt
through the credit union door and gets in line behind me,
    a woman who married a friend of mine,
married him twice, actually, because they married and divorced
    and remarried and are about to redivorce,
because all the things she couldn't stand about him
    the first time are things

she *really* can't stand now, plus there's a whole new list
    of character flaws, moral shortcomings,
intellectual debits, irritating table manners, facial tics,
    and shoulder twitches
that either she didn't notice before or that he has acquired
    since the first go-round,
not to mention those late-night thigh-muscle spasms of his
    that leave her sleepless

and thus doubly cantankerous from the moment she lays eyes
    on him in the morning
until the last disgusted stare she gives him at night
    as he lies next to her, eyes closed,
legs convulsing like those of Count Galvani's frog
    as the celebrated scientist-nobleman
slips the juice to him, mouth pursed in the O from which,
    soon, snores will issue,

and she's hanging over her husband's face
    and waiting for him to add snoring

to his other crimes and just hating the liver out of him,
    even though he loved her once to distraction,
couldn't get enough of her, and she liked him okay,
    but then she started finding fault
with this, fault with that, fault with me,
    whom she sees as a bad influence,

a guy who drinks too much and tricks her husband
    into doing the same, and now
she's behind me in line at the credit union,
    and I'm about to wet my pants
because I've been afraid of this woman for so long
    and wondering now if she's going
to shatter what a student of mine once described in an essay
    as "the thin vermeer of civilization"

and jump on my back and ride me across the lobby
    of the FSU Credit Union and knock my teeth out
against the counter as the tellers yank the cash out of the way
    and the customers hightail it for the door.
Sometimes I think we get around in our married lives
    the way Ray Charles did
when he used to drive in Tallahassee—old-timers have told me
    he'd room near the club where he was playing

and he'd memorize where he had to go and people
    would see him coming
and get out of the way or else shout, "Left, Ray!
    No, right, Ray,
rightrightright! That's it, man, you got it!" And him
    not seeing a thing but getting there
anyway and playing his set and then climbing in the car
    and driving home again.

When I was a college freshman, I fell hard for this senior
    whose name was Linda Fullilove
(I tell no lie), who was this irresistible combination
    of Cajun-country *volupté*
and buttoned-down cracker propriety, but she had a boyfriend,

so I never asked her out,
even though I became her confidant, sort of the way a knight
    becomes a queen's confidant

because he knows he's beneath her, and she does, too, and once
    Linda told me her psych class
had gone on a field trip to the nervous hospital
    over in Jackson, and as the professor
and the students were walking to the main gate, this drooler
    had come up to the fence
and whipped it out, "and if all men look like that,"
    Linda said, "I'm never getting married,"

and at the time I thought she meant if all men's penises looked
    like that, but later I wondered if she wasn't referring
to the whole picture—the dopey grin, the feet-apart stance,
    the firm overhand grip—though if she picked the right guy,
which, by the way, I never thought was her senior boyfriend,
    a disdainful milksop of a fellow more infatuated
with his own bland charms than with the musky deliciousness
    of what I thought of as the real Linda Fullilove,

the one operating just below the alluringly icy exterior
    of the Linda the world knew and gazed at longingly—
if she picked the right guy, she wouldn't mind,
    she'd even want to see him that way.
Or, like me, in line, with my friend's soon-to-be-ex-again
    burning laser-beam hate-holes in my back,
she too could end up asking herself, Is it them,
    is it this vast tribe of ex- and recycled lovers

and husbands and sweethearts and all their quondam beaux and belles,
    or is it me? How do we pick these people
and they us? What do they see when they look at us and we them?
    How do we become a Tige or a Sug Watley
or a Tige Watley's whoah? Here's another Victor Hugo quote for you,
    this time from Jean Cocteau: "Victor Hugo was a madman who
thought he was Victor Hugo." And I think I am myself, and he is himself,
    and she, she thinks she is herself, and you are you.

TEACHER OF THE YEAR

This year last year's Teacher of the Year
       broke an office window having sex with a student
at Laurie's university, Laurie tells me,
       and I say, "Ummm . . . broke it with what?"
and she says that's what everybody wants to know,
       like, the head? The booty? The consensus is

it was a foot bobbing UP and down and UP
       and down and then lashing out in a final ecstatic
spasm, crash! Then comes surprise, giggles,
       and shushing noises. Somebody finds out,
though. Somebody always finds out:
       my first Mardi Gras, when I was ten,

I remember passing a man saying,
       "Oh, come on, baby, why can't we let BY-gones
be BY-gones?" and shaking his cupped hands
       as though he is comparison-shopping
for coconuts while peering pleadingly
       into the pinched face of his female companion,

whose own arms are folded tightly across her chest,
       and even then I thought, Hmmm! Bet I know
what those bygones are! I.e., that they have
       nothing to do with who ate that last piece of cake
or brought the car home with the gas tank empty
       and everything to do with sex stuff.

Laurie is in town with Jack, who is a therapy dog,
       and she tells me she takes Jack to homes
and nursing centers to cheer up old-timers,
       and after their first visit, she asked
the activities coordinator if she should do
       anything differently, and the woman says,

"Could you dress him up?" and Laurie says,
        "Excuse me?" and the woman says,
"They really like it when the dogs wear clothes."
        My analysis: having seen people act like dogs
all their lives, toward the end, elderly folks
        find it amusing when dogs act like people.

A German shepherd could be Zorro, for example,
        and a chow Elvis as a matador. A poodle could be
St. Teresa of Avila, a border collie Sinatra.
        A yorkie could be a morris dancer
and a sheltie a gandy dancer or vice versa.
        A schnauzer could be Jayne Mansfield.

Dogs could pair up: imagine a boxer
        as Inspector Javert chasing a bassett hound
as Jean Valjean under the beds, around
        the potted plants, in and out of the cafeteria.
Or a bichon frisé as Alexander Hamilton fighting
        a duel with a Boston terrier as Aaron Burr.

On the romantic side, there could be
        a golden Lab and a chocolate Lab
as Romeo and Juliet or a samoyed and a husky
        as Tristan and Isolde, though it wouldn't be good
to let their love end the way doggie love does:
        the posture isn't nice, and the facial expressions

are not the kind of thing you want to think about
        when you're thinking about this kind of thing.
Up to a point, you want to know it all,
        then the more you know, the less you want to know.
Though you can't help wondering:
        A shoulder? An elbow? A knee?

FOR MEN ONLY

Emily, the deaf-and-blind shih tzu of our dear friend Victoria,
        is walking the hardwood floors
of this W. 12th Street apartment at four A.M., her nails tapping out
                a message TO: DEAF AND BLIND DOGS
OF THE WORLD (dit-dit-dot-dot-dit-dit-dit-dit)

FROM: EMILY (dit-dot-dot-dit-dot-dit-dot-dot-dit-dit-dot)
        ACTION: PEE ON THE FLOOR—NOW!
A famous painter's nephew lives across the way, and his sons
                have these beer parties
when the folks are away and throw up off the roof,

so on a given summer evening, you *might* go to sleep to the sound
        of the famous painter's grandnephews
throwing up off the roof and you will *definitely* wake
                to Emily's senescent jazz-tap routines,
like those of a doggie Judy Garland in *Babes on Broadway*

doing an endless series of spastic ball changes and waiting
        for her Mickey Rooney to appear
in the form of a schnauzer or airedale, an unlikely event, since—
                well, I was going to say that no dog
will love her now, but then there's that whole syndrome

scientists call Davian behavior, the relentless sex drive noticed,
        for example, in the *Bufo marinus* frog,
those three-pounders you see hopping down Miami sidewalks
                like little suitcases and the males
of which species have been observed having intercourse

in the middles of busy highways with females
        who are not only dead
but have been flattened by the tires of vehicles tearing past
                while old Warty has his grim, lusty way
with what was once surely the fair Esmeralda,

an enchanting voluptuary then but now a crusty fly-magnet
        on the asphalt, a transformation
overlooked by the amphibian gallant whose behavior was described
        in scientific literature, first jocularly,
then permanently, as Davian, so *à propos* is this term

for boundless lust that takes its name from the limerick
        about the hermit named Dave /
who kept a dead whore in his cave / and had to admit / I'm a bit
        of a shit / but think of the money, etc.
It gets better—or worse, depending on whether you're looking at it

from the linguistic or the moral viewpoint—for Davian behavior
        among birds is called Avian Davian behavior. . . .
Hmmm. To paraphrase what Maréchal Bosquet said about the charge
        of the Light Brigade, *C'est magnifique,*
mais ce n'est pas l'amour. Oh, love, love, what the hell is it anyway?

Victoria loves John, her new husband, but she doesn't love Emily,
        this old crazy dog
who wanders the apartment at night like Lady Macbeth,
        not incarnadining the multitudinous seas
with Duncan's blood but jaundicing Victoria's carpets and our socks.

Love's got a Paolo-and-Francesca part, a can't-keep-my-hands-off-
        my-baby, an if-loving-you-is-wrong-
I-don't-want-to-be-right side, but also a rational aspect,
        an emotion-recollected-in-tranquility component,
both of which I recall from the rhythm and blues of my youth

with its spraddle-legged shouters, yeah, but the calm guys, too,
        their voices smooth as cane syrup
as they sing, All you fellows, gather 'round me,
        I'm going to give you some good advice!
Sleepless, I am in Chinatown early next morning, gazing at the signs

and realizing I can't tell if I'm about to enter
        a Christian Science Reading Room

or a brothel, so I press my face against storefront windows
    and finally see people buying pills
and powders across a counter and go in, and the guy scowls at me

and I say I'm tired, I want something for energy,
    and he reaches behind himself
and picks up this box and bangs it down on the counter and says,
        You take For Men Only,
and I say, What's in it? and he says, You take For Men Only now!

So I start down the street with my bottle of For Men Only
    and open it and shake out a capsule
in my hand, and it's long and orange and has green spots
        like spinach and it smells the way
the yard does after you mow it, so I take one, and turn into,

I don't know, Garth Brooks. . . . I'm running all over the place,
    not feeling amorous so much
as wanting to, say, re-roof the house. I mean, I'm an older guy
        who's got it under control,
but pass this stuff out to the male population in general,

and every New York street corner would look like Bat Day
    at Yankee Stadium. Farewell to chastity!
If such a thing exists. And farewell to peace of mind, for sure.
        The chastest bachelor I know
is my son Will's hermit crab, who lives by himself in a terrarium

and eats nothing but candy, those marshmallow Easter chicks, specifically—
    oh, he'll take a little spinach dip,
if there's nothing else, but he'd rather have the candy,
        which he eats with a single spindly feeler.
He's as dainty as a maid, this crab, and might even be a maid,

but whatever he is, he brooks no nonsense from the succession
    of crab roommates Will has presented him with,
at least one of which must be of the opposite gender, but with all

of whom he has made war, not love.
He'd rather have that candy, and who's to say he's wrong,

for if you can't have everything the way you want, at least
        you should be able to have a snack.
Quite frankly, I don't think he's really trying, but then that's his business,
        not mine. The people I know
who are lucky at love are pretty good at slinging it themselves,

and this includes both virtuous people and sleazeball lounge-lizard types,
        cut-rate Romeos who come on
with the Barry White tapes and that junk about loving somebody
        and then setting them free—
I mean, why would you want to be free of someone who loves you to pieces?

I hate to keep paraphrasing the French, but why not, almost everything
        sounds better in French,
because it's another language, and though we'll never be able to reproduce
        the precise sense of the original,
that's okay, because we're talking about poetry here, not science,

and far from being harmed by lacunae and uncertainties,
        poetry is actually helped by them,
so here goes: *La beauté sera convulsive ou ne sera pas,*
        said Andre Breton, and let love too
be convulsive or let it not be at all. Chaps, let us rise above the hermit crabs

and hermits and old blind dogs, for when we invent our truest selves,
        the lovers we deserve will appear.
Therefore let us learn another language. Let us set our hair on fire
        and charge into battle against a numberless foe.
Let us sail upriver. Let us eat shit, drink blood, choke on pleasure.

I hear America singing; it sounds like Little Richard.
        He says, When she winks an eye,
the bread slice turn to toast, and I dream of Jayne Mansfield.
        He says, When she smiles, the beefsteak
become well-done, and I dream of Mamie Van Doren, Cyd Charisse.

Across the way, the famous painter's grandnephews
        vomit off the roof as Emily dances
through the night, hearing nothing, seeing nothing, though she too
        dreams of her lover:
Cerberus, guardian of hell, a dog's dog, three-headed and immortal.

in a little silver boat

The cab pulls up in front of our new apartment
on the Ile St-Louis to the unmistakable sounds
       of the *rite amoureux* filling the courtyard,
the woman crying, "Uh, uh, uh, ah oui, AH OUI, AH OUI!"
     as I try to count out the money to the taxi driver

     and go, "Okay, ninety, a hundred, a hundred, dammit,"
and him going, "Just start over," and me going, "Eighty,
       eighty-five, uh, eighty, eighty-five,"
and the driver finally waving me off impatiently
     and taking the bills out of my hands one at a time

     and holding them up, saying, "See, a hundred francs.
And ten for a tip, okay?" and me saying, "Okay!" to him
       and then, to Barbara as we drag the suitcases
up the stairs, "Did you hear that woman having
     that huge orgasm?" and Barbara saying, "Or faking it."

     In the months that we lived in that apartment
we were never even sure who the Ah Oui Girl was,
       though we narrowed down the list
of candidates to this one sort of blondish person
     in her twenties who usually looked seriously

     out of sorts, figuring surely anybody that grumpy
has the ability to turn on a dime and become
       une vraie tigresse, as I once heard a guy
on the *métro* describe his own girlfriend.
     But mainly we were having one terrific time in Paris:

     so many fabulous restaurants! We didn't know
what everything was, yet we ate it anyway, all of it,
       from *aiguillette* and *bourride*
to *loup au fenouil* and *méchoui* to *potiron* and *sandre*
     and *tourteaux,* grilledbroiledboiledroastedfried.

And that was before cheese and dessert.
And opera and dance and concerts and plays—
            we saw Racine's *Phèdre* three times, in fact,
once in English and once as a one-man show and then again
        with a full cast, only in French this time.

        The best part about being in Paris, though,
was that I could spend all this time with Barbara,
            walking along and talking or just sitting
at a little table over an Armagnac or a coffee
        and saying nothing, and we went out every night,

        and sometimes, as we crossed the courtyard on our way
back in, we'd hear the Ah Oui Girl—that was
            Barbara's name for her, the Ah Oui Girl—
and her boyfriend going at it,
        and often in the last days of summer

        there were flashes of what some people call
heat lightning, which is just other people's real lightning:
        we see it, but it's so far away
that we can't hear the thunder, and we turn our palm up,
        but we can't feel the rain,

        yet it's so hot out there, so we tell ourselves
the lightning is caused by the heat, i.e., by something
        it isn't caused by at all.
One night we came in and these huge bolts were flashing
        silently high over the ancient crenellations

        and cries of "ah oui, ah oui, AH OUI!"
were bouncing off the courtyard walls;
        we'd had maybe a little too much
to drink, and as we headed toward our staircase,
        Barbara said, "They're going at it again!"

        just a little too loudly, and they stopped for a moment,
but by the time we got upstairs,

they'd started afresh, and we opened the windows
and listened to them for a while—
        listened to her, I mean—and then made love ourselves.

        Quietly, though. I would have been embarrassed
for either of us to make noise like the Ah Oui Girl,
                though I envied her enthusiasm
and wished I could relax and just let myself go more
        and not be so, uh, obsessive about everything.

        I wanted to be more like her, even though
I didn't know who she was—I mean, I knew who she was
                when I could hear her, but only then.
Once Barbara suggested that since we'd never identified her
        conclusively, maybe she didn't exist,

        that maybe her boyfriend was an Ah Oui Guy,
a countertenor who did her voice so that everyone
                would think he was a great lover, a kind of fourth-
arrondissement Norman Bates with sex on his mind,
        not stabbing Janet Leigh to death.

        Another reason I was glad to be in Paris
was because at last I was able to read as much
                as I wanted to, and Barbara, too,
and since I was intensely interested in a woman
        both bookish and beautiful and saw reading

        as one more connection to her, in fact, saw it
as indispensable to love, I wondered if the Ah Oui Girl
                was bookish as well or if she and her boyfriend
went at it with sheer animal passion, if theirs was just
        pure screaming brainless hormonal wall-socket sex,

        and one chilly night just before we leave I take a walk
and come in to the sounds of the Ah Oui Girl having
                her usual carefree good time, and Barbara says,

"Did you hear the Ah Oui Girl and her boyfriend?"
	and as I get in bed I say, "I heard the Ah Oui Girl,"

	and the next thing I know, the sun is coming up
and I'm going out to get the mail, and when I turn around,
		I bump into somebody and say, *"Pardon,"*
and it's the Ah Oui Girl, and I say, *"Bonjour, mademoiselle,"*
	and she scowls, and I think, Um, maybe that's not her.

ROMAN POLANSKI'S COOKIES

One night I come back from the library late
     and there are all these floodlights
on the Quai de Bourbon, where we live, and there is
       this big table with all these cookies on it
and these big bottles of mineral water,

so I ask somebody what's going on, and he tells me
     Roman Polanski is shooting a scene from a new movie
of his called *The Ninth Gate,* so I hang around
       for a while and soon Roman Polanski shows up,
and he has this big cigar in his face,

and it sure doesn't look like a King Edward!
     But then I notice that there are these
chocolate-covered graham crackers
       on the cookie table that look like the ones
I used to love when I was a kid, and even though the cookies

are obviously for the actors, I can't help sneaking one,
     and it turns out to be exactly the cookie
I'm thinking of, and since by this time the actors
       have shown up and are rehearsing their scene
and showing no interest whatsoever in the cookies,

I take another and another, and soon I'm hog-facing
     those cookies like nobody's business, only
just then I look up, and there's Roman Polanksi
       standing there with that big cigar in his hand
and staring at me with a look of pure hatred, as if to say,

"Stop eating all those goddamned chocolate-covered
     graham crackers!" And while part of me
wants to say, "Make your movie, dude, it's only a cookie,"
       another part of me realizes that maybe they're
his favorite cookies, too, and that even while

he was blocking out the scene and moving lights around
         and giving the actors their cues, what he'd really
been obsessing on was those chocolate-covered graham
                  crackers, same as me,
though who's to say? Who, including ourselves,

knows what we know and when we know it? A few years ago
         Barbara and I were at this dinner party,
and this scientist woman kept wanting to know how
             I wrote poetry and how I knew if it was good
or not, and I said, "Well, experience helps a lot,"

and she said if experience was all there was to it,
         then we could find a cure for cancer tomorrow,
and I said I didn't say experience was all there was to it,
             just that it helped a lot, and that as far as
knowing whether a poem was good or not, it was good

if an editor accepted it, so she wanted to know
         how the editor knew if it was good or not
in an objective, i.e., quantifiable, sense,
             and I'm doing my best to stay polite,
but just then her scientist husband joins her,

and the two of them begin to raise their voices,
         and even though I haven't said anything about
all the dumb science that's done out there as well as
             the faked science, not to mention
the evil science, suddenly they're mad at me,

or maybe they're really mad at poetry.
         Maybe Roman Polanski hates me because
I'm taller than he is. Maybe Roman Polanski hates himself.
             Everybody hates somebody:
we cast about for the author of our misery, and lo, it is us.

A friend who's just come back from Alba, in Italy,
         says Beppe Scavini the candymaker

has gone back to the wife he told everyone was so ugly.
                    So now he has to say: "She's not ugly!
She's beautiful! I never said she was ugly!"

Oh, and in 1991, I gave this reading in Princeton,
                    and the guy who was my host told me he'd bought
this particular species of dog,
                    but after a couple of years the dog sickened
and died, which is when the vet told him

that the dog he'd thought was about four
                    when he bought him was actually closer
to ten years old and that the breeder had lied.
                    And then the same thing happened again!
Different breeder, different dog, but same species,

and once again he'd bought what he'd thought
                    was a young dog, only to see it turn gray
and blurry-eyed before its time. Then the guy telling
                    the story says, "Oh, well, as crimes go,
I suppose that's not so bad, is it?" and I say, "What?"

and he says, "Lying about the ages of dogs," and I say,
                    "What do you mean?" and he says, "You know,
compared to arson or genocide. . . ." But it's more
                    than a lie, I wanted to say, it's depriving a man
of the love of his dog, surely the purest love there is,

but then I see the guy had looked at his memory and looked
                    and looked at it until he found a handle
he could pick it up with, so who am I to murder his peace
                    of mind? There's so much we can't find
a handle for, so much like those little gardens with hedges

and gravel walks or courtyards with birds and fountains
                    that I've seen from one window or another both here
in Paris and in Italy, too, yet when
                    you leave your building and go into the street,
you look and look for them, and they're not there.

EXCELLENT WOMEN

There's something about a woman with an automatic weapon,
      I'm thinking in the Auditorium du Louvre,
because as I wait for the concert to begin, the musicians
      are hurrying down the aisles with
those over-the-shoulder nylon cases that must protect
      the violins better and are easier
to carry, too, though I can't help waxing nostalgic
      for the old-school Machine Gun Kelly–type

wooden cases, which reminds me of the Bastille Day parade
      we'd seen on the Champs-Elysées
a few weeks earlier and all the handsome soldiers there,
      many of them women who were
very well turned-out and well-armed to boot:
      the carefully tailored trousers
showing haunch and *derrière* to best effect,
      the nurturing bosom that a sobbing general

might lay his head on, and then the gun she can
      shoot everybody to death with!
Just BA-DA-DA-DA-DA-DA-DA! A smiling crowd turned
      into a heap of bloody giblets!
Though that's not how the woman herself sees it,
      I'm sure. More likely, she sees herself
as disciplined, empowered, and so on. Full of
      mental fight. Mastering negative emotions.

The book I'm reading as I wait for the music to start
      is on the famous case of the *Mary Celeste,*
which left New York for Genoa on November 7, 1872, with
      Captain Benjamin Spooner Briggs aboard
and his wife Sarah and a crew of eight as well as a cargo
      of alcohol and would be found off the coast
of Portugal by the *Deo Gratia* on December 4, provisioned
      and in good order but deserted.

Mr. Frederick Solly Flood, Queen's Surveyor at Gibraltar,
      will speculate that the crew had got
at the liquor and, "in the fury of drunkeness," murdered
      everyone aboard, themselves included.
That being the case, why did the ship appear "fit to go
      around the world," as a seaman aboard
the *Deo Gratia* said? Also, what exactly is "the fury of
      drunkeness"? It sounds like something

a high-toned Christian would say and not a true state
      of mind. What is more likely is that some
of the alcohol leaked from its barrels into the sealed hold,
      which, when opened, gave out either an uprush
of malodorous fumes or a roaring noise or both.
      Getintheboatgetintheboat! says Captain Briggs
to his wife and crew, who are having a bad day—their last,
      in fact, though they don't know that yet.

A person might ask why Captain Briggs and the others
      didn't return to the ship after a while
when they saw there was nothing really wrong on board,
      but a thoughtful person might ask
a better question, namely, what are the mental states
      of those in the lifeboat, probably
16 to 20 feet long with no more than 9 to 12 inches
      of freeboard—that is to say,

not *what is happening to them* but *what are they thinking?*
      Is Sarah Briggs thinking of the dream
she'd had that morning, or not a dream, exactly, but
      a mind-picture she saw upon waking briefly
and then sleeping again and then, in a moment neither
      wakeful nor sleeping yet partaking of both states
simultaneously, looking into her husband's ear and seeing,
      for the first time, the inside of his head?

It was like a forest in there, with big curved bones
      instead of trees and, in the middle,

a clearing that was at the same time sunny and fog-filled.
          That's when she knew they didn't have a chance,
because a man with a mind like that would be spirited yet
          equivocal in a time of crisis.
Now she hates her husband, hates him to death.
          Then she makes herself think of the little melodeon

she'd brought on board and of her attempts to play preludes
          and fugues and sonatas yet having to turn
instead, not because of her lack of skill but because of
          the instrument's limitations, to hymns
and dirges and church music—"Nearer My God to Thee" and
          that sort of thing. And this is when Sarah Briggs
feels what Whitman calls "the peace and knowledge
          that pass all the argument of the earth."

Oh, look, the house lights are going down. Mental states
          often being infectious, let's fervently
wish for each of them handshakes and embraces all around:
          Good-bye, Benjamin! Good-bye, Sarah, so firm
of purpose and outlook! Good-bye, men! Good-bye, good-bye!
          The *Mary Celeste* is rapidly retreating toward
the horizon, and already they see themselves in their
          angel bodies, their flight as liquid as any music.

MODERATION KILLS (EXCUSEZ-MOI, JE SUIS SICK AS A DOG)

I'm tackling this particularly chewy piece of sushi and
          recalling the only Japanese words I know,
"Fugu wa kuitashii, inochi wa oshishii," meaning,
          "I would like to eat fugu—but live!"
which, I've read, is something Japanese executives say
          when contemplating a particularly risky

course of action, because whereas the testes of the fugu
          or blowfish are harmless
yet highly prized as a virility builder, the liver,
          which is almost identical
in appearance to the testes, is toxic, so that
          a less-cautious individual,

a fisherman, say, who thinks himself as skillful
          as the chef who has actually been
educated and licensed in the preparation of fugu,
          might eat the wrong organ and die,
face-down in his rice bowl, chopsticks nipping
          spasmodically at the air.

Coming in from the vegetable patch, the fisherman's wife
          sees him cooling in the remains
of his meal and shrieks, and I don't know
          the Japanese for this,
"You have eaten fugu—and died!" True, though
          for anyone other than the new widow,

why should his death be exclaimed upon as though
          it were a failure or defeat,
since the fisherman had finished a good day of work
          and was not only enjoying his tasty snack
but also looking forward to the enhancement
          of his powers of generation,

this being therefore a fine moment in which to expire
        and certainly preferable to
countless moments of life as a fumbling drooler
        (since fugu liver can paralyze
as well), a burden to his loved ones as well as
        the object of their contempt.

Then someone across the table from me says he's *heard*
        of a state of mind called boredom
but never actually experienced it, and I wonder,
        Can a mind that never sinks
into the cold gray waters of boredom ever rise to
        the blue-and-gold heavens of ecstasy?

Then someone else shouts, "Excusez-moi, je suis sick
        as a dog!" and disappears
laughing, but that's okay, because "ecstasy" =
        "ex stasis" = "get off the dime" =
"fish or cut bait" = "lead, follow, or get out
        of the way," does it not?

Besides, who's to say the fisherman didn't hate
        his wife, couldn't stand her?
And had to eat fugu testes in order to be able
        to countenance her and
therefore is better off dead and unknowing than
        alive and fully sentient of such misery?

Or hated himself and therefore is better off dead, etc.?
        And therefore who is
more admirable, the executive who fears death
        or the fisherman who actually dies?
Does the former feel brave merely because
        he has *talked* of taking a risk?

Would the doughty fisherman have said "Fugu wa kuitashii,
        inochi wa oshishii" and taken pride
in his temperance? Certainly not—

offered the same challenge under identical
circumstances, he'd have said, and I don't know
    the Japanese for this either, "Moderation kills."

MY DEAD DAD

Our Rue Albert apartment has this pre-Napoleonic water heater
      that lurches to life with a horripilating bang
when, for example, Barbara is taking a bath, as she is now,
      and every time she turns the handle for
more hot water, the heater hesitates a second, then ka-pow!

as though there's a little service technician sitting inside
      working a crossword, his elbows on his knees,
and suddenly he gets the more-hot-water signal and jumps up
      off his little doll-house chair and runs down
the walkway and throws a shovelful of coal in the furnace

and then walks back, wiping his brow, only to have Barbara
      crank that faucet again, and thwack! he's off
and running while I'm sitting in our French living room
      reading *Journey to the End of Night* by Céline,
whose prose is sweaty and overheated in the first place,

when boom! there he goes once more, sprinting toward
      the furnace, and Barbara is giving
these little cries of either pleasure or surprise or both,
      as she does when bathing, and ba-boom!
there he goes. I imagine him in neatly pressed khakis

and a shirt to match and a hat with a patent-leather brim,
      in the manner of the gas-station attendants
I remember from the days of my youth, and I wonder if he
      is not a relative of the equally little man
in the refrigerator whose job it was, according to my dad,

to turn the light on whenever anyone opened the refrigerator
      door and off when they closed it
and who, in my child's mind, bore a striking resemblance
      to my dad not only in appearance
but also patience and love of word games and other nonsense.

And if there is such a little man in my French refrigerator
       and water heater and one
in my refrigerator and water heater back home,
       and if there are five billion of
us big people in the world, there must be twenty billion of them!

I think, like us, they'd have entertainments, such as
       circuses, barbecues, and *thés dansants,*
but also wars and horrible acts of cruelty!
       Though when peace returned, entire towns of
little people would finish the evening meal and then go on

the *passeggiata* the way the Italians do, the young flirting,
       the old sighing as they admire and envy the young,
the children and dogs getting mixed up in everybody's legs
       as they stroll and chat and ready themselves for
sleep as the clock in the little clock tower strikes eleven,

twelve, one, and the moon comes up—the moon! Which also
       has its little men, according to my dad,
though these are green and, to our eyes, largely invisible,
       since they live on the dark half,
though every once in a while they, too, become curious,

and a few will sneak over into the glary, sunlit side,
       so that when the moon is full, he said,
we should stare at it with every optical instrument at our
       disposal, because if we do, we just might see
one of those little fellows nibbling the piece of cheese

he holds in one hand as he shields his eyes with the other
       and squints down at us. And I haven't even got
to the good little people who live inside each bad one
       of us, according to pop psychologists,
though I don't think my dead dad would have bought that one,

yet since the few people left who knew us both often say
       how much I remind them of him, then I think

if my dead dad lives anywhere at all, he lives inside me.
	Well, and my brother, too, if not
our mother, though there's nothing unusual about that,

because the older I get, the more widows I know, and
	none of them ever says anything about
her dead husband, suggesting perhaps these champions
	weren't so fabulous after all, at least
to them. Sad thought, isn't it, that these men should live

only in the minds of their children. Or maybe my dead dad's
	on the moon, since the alternate point
of view to my smug phenomenological one is that people
	go to heaven when they die,
and heaven's in the sky, and the moon's in the sky,

so who's to say that's not my dead dad up there, his mouth
	full of limburger or provolone,
shielding his eyes as he tries to find the house
	where we used to live, but he can't,
because it's been torn down, though he'd have no way

of knowing that, so he looks for my mother, and she's there,
	but she lives in a retirement community now,
and he can't believe how old she is, and he's shocked that
	she's as beautiful as he always knew
her to be, only she can't walk now, can't hear, can't see.

And he looks for my brother in Ohio, and he's there,
	and me in Florida, where he left me,
but I'm not there anymore. Hey, Dad! Over here! In France!
	No, France! Great country! Great cheese.
I wish I could take you in my pocket with me everywhere I go.

THE EXORCIST OF NOTRE-DAME

Just after we get to Paris I learn that there's an exorcist
        at Notre-Dame named Père Nicolas, and when I stop by,
sure enough, there he is with his name tag on,
                a chubby white-haired guy taking to an elderly lady
who doesn't look at all as though she thinks

the Seine is filled with blood or the College of Cardinals
        is a bunch of scaly Komodo dragons flicking their tongues
around and electing Beelzebub pope, and while I'd like to
                hang out and watch the people to see if the ones
with demons turn their heads around backward and say,

"Yugga-ugga-mooga-waaga-aaga!" when they walk by
        or if their tee shirts begin to writhe as though a couple
of rattlesnakes are having seizures just before Père Nicolas
                jumps up to put the double whammy woo-woo juju on them,
I need to get home so we can make an 8:30 booking

at the Square Trousseau, and in the restaurant there's a youngish woman
        sitting next to us with an older guy
who reminds me of my dead father, and they're quiet,
                as father and daughter have a right to be, and he's eating well,
even if he seems a little bored by the whole thing,

a little downcast, though he looks up at me after a while
        and then down again and then up rather sharply,
as though he recognizes me, and a little smile crosses his face
                for just an instant. And there's another table behind ours
with six drunk Brits talking football at the top of their lungs,

though they're so drunk and they have so much food
        in their mouths that they sound like jackals or bears
who've only made it through the first two weeks
                of the human-conversation class: "Ugga-wooga-
agga-hagga-MANCHESTER UNITED!-agga-mugga-

wugga-ARSENAL!-oogga!" So the old guy and his daughter
        get dessert, and Barbara and I our main courses, while the Brits
bark and snap at each other, and the old guy keeps looking at me,
            and when the check arrives, the daughter pays,
and he comes over and says, "Enjoy your meal?" and he sounds the way

my dad would have sounded if my dad had been French,
        and he tilts his head toward the noisy table and says,
"They're a bit noisy, don't you think?"
            and he's so much like my dad that I feel my jaw
begin to quiver and tears start down my face, and the old guy puts his hand

on my shoulder and says, "Don't cry. I have good news for you,"
        and for a moment I'm convinced that it is my dad,
that he has news for me from the other side, that it's nice over there,
            always sunny and cool, and you can get anything you want
to eat, and that he's got this great place, it's like a house

in one of those medieval woodcuts that's open to the world,
        with a river on one side and a winding road on the other,
and one day my mother will come up that road,
            and then my older brother, and then me,
and he tilts his head toward the Brits and says,

"It could be worse," and I'm so ashamed of my tears
        that all I can say is, "H-how?" and he leans a little closer
and jacks his eyebrows a couple of times and says,
        "They could have cell phones," and, well, no, it isn't my dad, is it,
there's probably not even an afterlife at all, is there,

nor demons, or at least no demons other than the ones
        who're there to dog us on the days when exhaustion or fear
has made us allergic to everyone, our own selves included,
            the days dead opposite to what Randall Jarrell called
"the day of our life," i.e., one with the right lunch, right music

and books and movies, right sweetheart, right friends.
        And I want to talk to Père Nicolas about all this,

but the sign outside his confessional says he speaks
            only German and Spanish and French, not English,
meaning I'd have to talk my strictly intermediate-level French

to him, about which I'm self-conscious enough already,
            not to mention—and I know this sounds stupid, but I've run out
of conditioner and can't find a French kind that works for me,
            so my hair is sticking out all over the place like that of
a "clown" (i.e., not a circus performer but Latin *colonnus*

or rube, clodhopper, mountain William, bumpkin,
            guy on a day pass), and there I'd be going, *"Pensez-vous,*
pensez, um, *c'est-à-dire,* uh, *pensez-vous,"* and later that night,
            as the priests are all sitting around the big oak dinner table
working on their *jarret de porc rôti* and their *daube à la provençale,*

the others, the older priests who're jealous or the modern ones
            who don't believe in demonic possession
in the first place, are kidding him and saying, "Run into
            any devils today, Père Nicolas?"
and he says "No, just a woman from Ghana

with stomach pains and a *monsieur* who thinks people
            are talking about him on the *métro*
and, uh, oh yeah! this stuttering sort of spastic hillbilly
            zombie hayseed type person who, well,
I really don't know what he wanted," and it could play out

that way, all cynical and funny and word-drunk,
            because in his line of work,
Père Nicolas would have to have a sense of humor, wouldn't he,
            or else he'd end up consulting one of the other
ninety-four licensed exorcists in France, though in his secret heart

I know he thinks my dad is right, my dead dad, that is,
            the real one, and that my real dad is up there
in that little house, and my mother and brother will come up
            that road to meet him, and in time, I'll come, too,
not on the road, but on the river, in a little silver boat.